First World War
and Army of Occupation
War Diary
France, Belgium and Germany

59 DIVISION
176 Infantry Brigade
South Staffordshire Regiment
2/6th (T.F.) Battalion
26 January 1916 - 26 February 1916

WO95/3021/8

The Naval & Military Press Ltd
www.nmarchive.com
Published in association with The National Archives

Published by

The Naval & Military Press Ltd

Unit 10 Ridgewood Industrial Park,

Uckfield, East Sussex,

TN22 5QE England

Tel: +44 (0) 1825 749494

www.naval-military-press.com

www.nmarchive.com

This diary has been reprinted in facsimile from the original. Any imperfections are inevitably reproduced and the quality may fall short of modern type and cartographic standards.

© **Crown Copyright**
Images reproduced by permission of The National Archives, London, England, 2015.

Contents

Document type	Place/Title	Date From	Date To
Heading	WO95/3021/8		
Heading	War Diary of 2/6th Batt South Staffs Regiment From 1st January 1916 To 31st January 1916 Volume 1		
War Diary	S. Albans	26/01/1916	29/01/1916
Heading	War Diary of 2/6th Battalion South Staffordshire Regiment From February 1st 1916 To February 29th 1916 (Volume II)		
War Diary	St Albans	14/02/1916	26/02/1916

WO 95/30218

Confidential

War Diary of

2/6th Batt South Staffs Regiment

from 1st January 1916 to 31st January 1916

Volume 1

Army Form C. 2118.

2/6 Batt. South Staffs Regt
WAR DIARY
INTELLIGENCE SUMMARY.
(Erase heading not required.)

Instructions regarding War Diaries and Intelligence Summaries are contained in F. S. Regs., Part II. and the Staff Manual respectively. Title pages will be prepared in manuscript.

Hour, Date, Place	Summary of Events and Information	Remarks and references to Appendices
26 January 1916 S.T ALBANS	100 Short M.L.E. Mark III* sighted H.V.A. Rifles received and 25 issued to each Company.	N.a.
29 January 1916 S.T ALBANS.	100 Recruits, enlisted under LORD DERBY'S scheme, were taken on the strength of this Battalion this week.	N.a.

H. Taylor
Lt. Colonel
Commanding 2/6 The South Staffs Regt

Confidential

War Diary

of

7/6th Battalion South Staffordshire Regiment

from February 1st 1916 to February 29th 1916

(Volume II)

2/6 Batt. South Stafford g-

WAR DIARY
or
INTELLIGENCE SUMMARY.
(Erase heading not required.)

Army Form C. 2118.

Hour, Date, Place	Summary of Events and Information	Remarks and references to Appendices
14th February 1916 ST ALBANS	Major General A.E. SANDBACH C.B. D.S.O. took over the command of the 2/1st NORTH MIDLAND DIVISION vice Major General R.M.R. READE C.B.	N/a
16th February 1916 ST ALBANS	Colonel (acting Brigadier-General) L.R. CARLETON took over the command of the 176th INFANTRY BRIGADE vice Colonel H.C. POLE-RELL.	N/a
26 February 1916 ST ALBANS.	243 Recruits, enlisted under LORD DERBY'S scheme, were taken in the strength of the Battalion this month making a total of 373 Recruits for the said strength and completing the present establishment of this Battalion of 850 men.	N/a

M. Albans.
29.2.16.

H. Taylor.
Lt Colonel.
Commanding 2/6 South Staffs R.t.